W9-BDX-350

AUG 2006

# BATS SET II

# LITTLE BROWN BATS

Jill C. Wheeler
ABDO Publishing Company

3 1150 01003 5265

BOISE PUBLIC LIBRARY

## visit us at
## www.abdopub.com

Published by ABDO Publishing Company, 4940 Viking Drive, Edina, Minnesota 55435.
Copyright © 2006 by Abdo Consulting Group, Inc. International copyrights reserved in all countries. No part of this book may be reproduced in any form without written permission from the publisher. The Checkerboard Library™ is a trademark and logo of ABDO Publishing Company.

Printed in the United States.

Cover Photo: © Merlin D. Tuttle, Bat Conservation International
Interior Photos: Animals Animals p. 13; Corbis pp. 5, 19; © Merlin D. Tuttle, Bat Conservation
 International pp. 9, 11, 17, 21

Series Coordinator: Tamara L. Britton
Editors: Tamara L. Britton, Stephanie Hedlund
Art Direction, Maps, and Diagrams: Neil Klinepier

### Library of Congress Cataloging-in-Publication Data

Wheeler, Jill C., 1964-
    Little brown bats / Jill C. Wheeler.
        p. cm. -- (Bats. Set II)
    Includes bibliographical references (p. ).
    ISBN 1-59679-325-2
     I. Title.

  QL737.C595W48 2005
  599.4'72--dc22
                                                    2005046531

# CONTENTS

# LITTLE BROWN BATS

There are more than 900 **species** of bats. Only rodents have more species. There are more than 300 species in the little brown bat's **family**.

In the United States, there are more little brown bats than any other bat species. These bats are also found in southern Canada and northern Mexico.

Like all bats, little brown bats are **mammals**. An amazing one-quarter of all mammals are bats. Humans are mammals, too. Mother bats produce milk to feed their young, just like human mothers. However, bats are the only mammals that truly fly.

Many people think bats are scary or harmful. But, bats are very helpful to humans. They eat many insect pests. Other bats help **pollinate** plants or plant new trees. Bats rarely harm humans or pets. They are an important part of Earth's **ecosystem**.

*A little brown bat roosts on a tree.*

# WHERE THEY'RE FOUND

Bats can be found all over the world. They live everywhere except for some **isolated** islands, and the North and South poles. Little brown bats live in North America. They are the the most common bat in the United States.

Little brown bats live in Alaska, southern Canada, most of the United States, and northern Mexico. They live in many **habitats**. These include forests, grasslands, and mountains.

Little brown bats are among the bat **species** that migrate. They live in warm areas in the summer. When the weather turns cold, they move to warmer climates to **hibernate**. They can migrate more than 200 miles (322 km) from one home to another. The bats return to their summer homes in the spring.

Little brown bats can adapt to a wide temperature range. They can **hibernate** in nearly freezing temperatures. They also can live where temperatures top 130 degrees Fahrenheit (54°C).

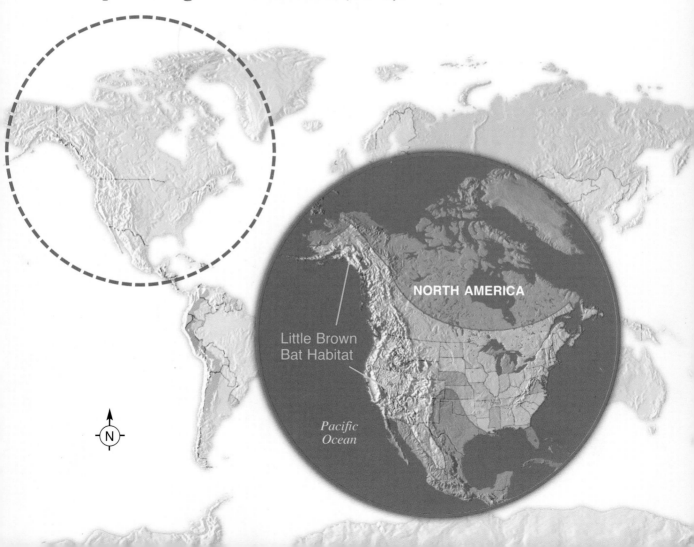

NORTH AMERICA

Little Brown Bat Habitat

Pacific Ocean

N

# WHERE THEY LIVE

Little brown bats live in a colony. During the summer, they **roost** in attics, under bridges, and in mines. They also find shelter under tree bark, in hollow trees, in rock **crevices**, or in caves. They like to live near water, where there are plenty of insects to eat!

In the winter, little brown bats migrate and find homes in caves or mines. The roost's temperature stays just above freezing all winter.

The bats **hibernate** close together in their winter home. Being near each other helps to slow water **evaporation** from their bodies. This keeps the bats from waking up thirsty. Waking up during hibernation uses much stored energy. If the bats use up their stored energy, they will not live until summer when food is available.

These little brown bats are hibernating. The drops of water on their fur are from the heat and moisture in the cave.

# SIZES

There are many sizes of bats. The smallest bat is the bumblebee bat. It is really the size of a big bumblebee!

The world's largest bats are the flying foxes. Some flying fox bats are more than 17 inches (43 cm) long. They can have a **wingspan** of more than 5 feet (1.5 m)!

Though little brown bats fall between these extremes, they are still small bats. Their bodies are about 3 and one-half inches (9 cm) long. They weigh as little as one-fourth of an ounce (7 g). That is about as much as a penny weighs. Their wingspan is 10 inches (25 cm).

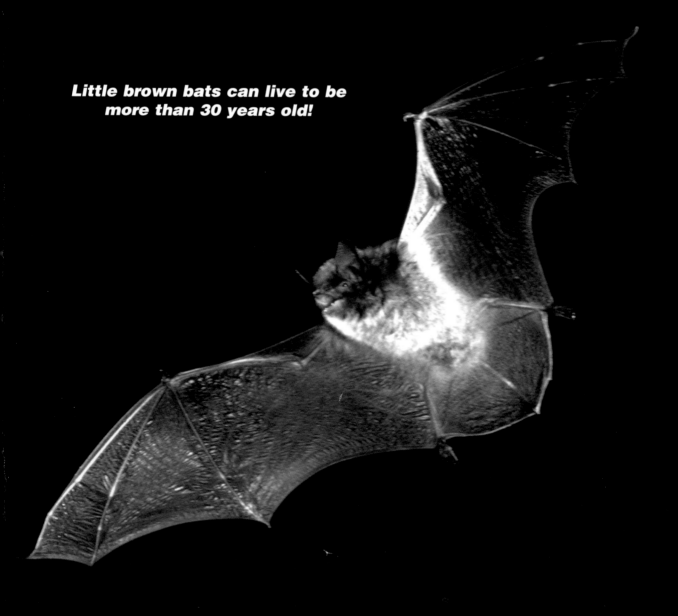

Little brown bats can live to be more than 30 years old!

# SHAPES

Little brown bats have long, glossy fur. It can be tan, reddish brown, or dark brown in color. They have long hairs on their toes. The hairs go beyond the tips of their claws!

On their head, little brown bats have small black ears with slightly pointed ear flaps. They have a plain nose. Two arms stretch from their small body. They have two hands. Each hand has four fingers and a thumb with a claw.

Stretched between the bat's fingers, body, and legs are **elastic** wing **membranes**. These membranes form the bat's wings. Little brown bats can fly up to 21 miles per hour (34 km/h). They average about 12 miles per hour (19 km/h).

# Bat Anatomy

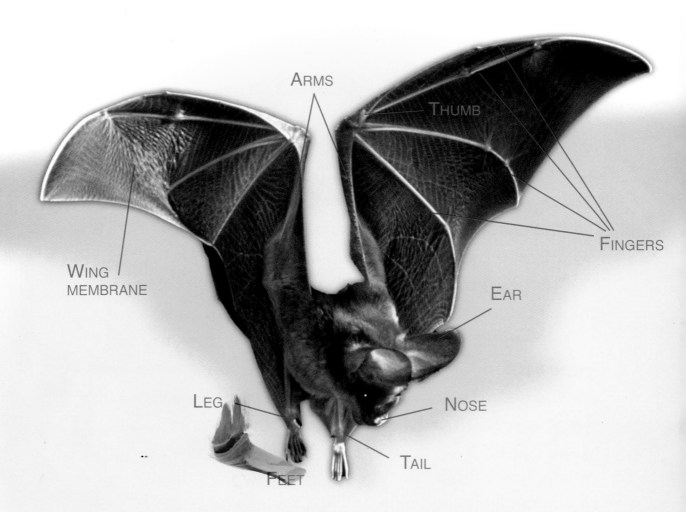

ARMS

THUMB

FINGERS

WING MEMBRANE

EAR

LEG

NOSE

FEET

TAIL

# Senses

Little brown bats are **nocturnal**. They come out at night to find food. You may have heard the phrase "blind as a bat." This rumor probably started because bats only come out at night. Yet bats can see. They can also hear, smell, taste, and feel. About half of all bats have another sense called echolocation. This is how bats "see" in the dark.

To use echolocation, bats make high-pitched sounds. Some bats make these sounds from their throat, and some from their nose. These sound waves go out and bounce off an object such as a tree, building, or insect.

The sound's echoes return to the bats. They catch the echoes in their ears. The bats use the echoes to locate objects. The echoes also tell the bats how big the objects are. Bats use echolocation to fly safely and to find food. They also use it to avoid danger.

**Sound wave sent out by bat**

**Echo wave received by bat**

# DEFENSE

Birds of **prey**, such as hawks and owls, like to eat little brown bats.  Raccoons, minks, and leopard frogs like to eat them, too.  Little brown bats seek out safe **roosting** places to hide from these **predators**.  The bats also use their flying skills and echolocation to avoid them.

But, little brown bats can't use echolocation to avoid all threats.  Humans are threatening the **habitat** of some little brown bats.

Little brown bats use caves to **hibernate**.  But, some caves have been turned into tourist spots.  Other caves are popular among spelunkers, which are people who like to explore caves.

Both of these things upset the bats.  Two species of little brown bats in the United States are now listed as **endangered** because of this human activity.

This old church building makes a safe roost for these little brown bats.

# FOOD

Little brown bats leave their **roosts** at night to hunt. They feed over water, forest trails, cliff faces, meadows, and farm fields. Little brown bats use echolocation to find insects. They like gnats, beetles, crane flies, wasps, moths, and mosquitoes.

When the little brown bats find an insect, they sweep it up with their wing tips. Then, the bug is transferred into a pouch formed by the tail and wing **membrane**.

The bats take the bug from their tail pouch into their mouth. Their sharp, pointy teeth do the rest. Little brown bats can chew 7 times per second. They can eat up to 1,200 bugs per hour. That's a lot of chewing!

Little brown bats have to get plenty to eat in the summer and fall. They must store up enough energy to live on through the winter. When they go into **hibernation**, about one-fourth of their body weight is fat.

This little brown bat is enjoying a katydid for supper!

# Babies

Fall is mating time for little brown bats. When spring comes, little brown bats return to their summer homes. There, a new generation of little brown bats is born between late May and mid-July.

The baby bats are called pups. Mother bats have one pup each year. They give birth with their heads up instead of hanging upside down. They catch the newborn pup in their tail pouch when it is born. The pup then begins to drink its mother's milk. Little brown bat pups open their eyes on their second day of life.

Baby bats are quite large when they are born. Little brown bats are about a quarter of the size of their mother at birth. And, their thumbs and hind feet are almost adult sized. This helps them cling to their mothers or to their **roost**.

*Little brown bat pups grow fast. Their wings get ten times bigger in just three weeks. Then they begin to learn to fly.*

Female little brown bats form colonies to raise their babies. Researchers have found nursery colonies of more than 5,000 bats. There, the bats are safe and warm. When they are about eight weeks old, they are grown adult bats. Soon, they will find mates of their own.

# GLOSSARY

**crevice** - a narrow crack into or through something.

**ecosystem** (EE-koh-sihs-tuhm) - a community of organisms and their environment.

**elastic** - able to return to normal shape after being stretched or bent.

**endangered** - in danger of becoming extinct.

**evaporate** - to change from a liquid or a solid into vapor.

**family** - a group that scientists use to classify similar plants or animals. It ranks above a genus and below an order.

**habitat** - a place where a living thing is naturally found.

**hibernate** - to spend the winter in an inactive state.

**isolate** - to separate from something.

**mammal** - an animal with a backbone that nurses its young with milk.

**membrane** - a thin, easily bent layer of animal tissue.

**nocturnal** (nahk-TUHR-nuhl) - active at night.

**pollinate** - when birds and insects transfer pollen from one flower or plant to another.

**predator** - an animal that kills and eats other animals.

**prey** - animals that are eaten by other animals; also, the act of seizing prey.

**roost** - a place, such as a cave or a tree, where bats rest during the day; also, to perch.

**species** (SPEE-sheez) - a kind or type.

**wingspan** - the distance from one wing tip to the other when the wings are spread.

# WEB SITES

To learn more about little brown bats, visit ABDO Publishing Company on the World Wide Web at **www.abdopub.com**. Web sites about bats are featured on our Book Links page. These links are routinely monitored and updated to provide the most current information available.

# INDEX